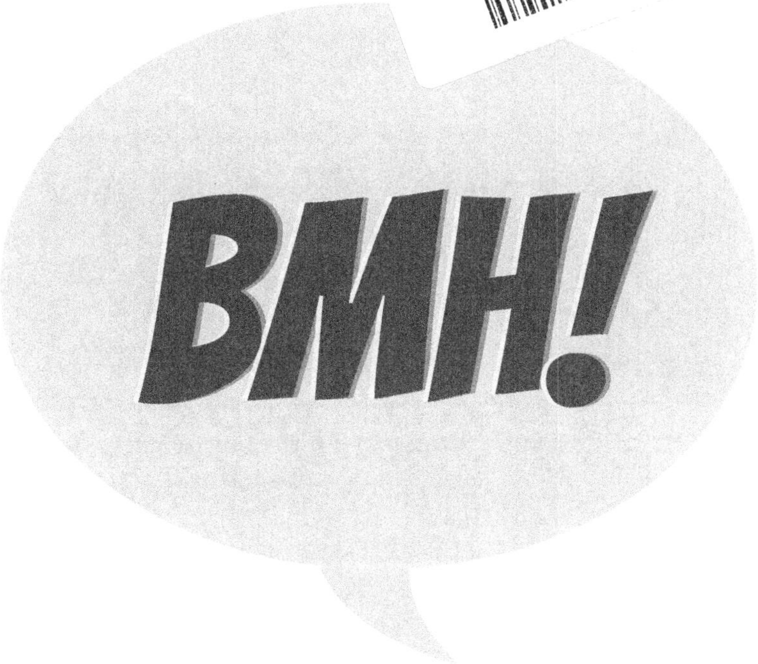
BMH!

BROKE MY HIP

TOT!

TEXTING ON TOILET

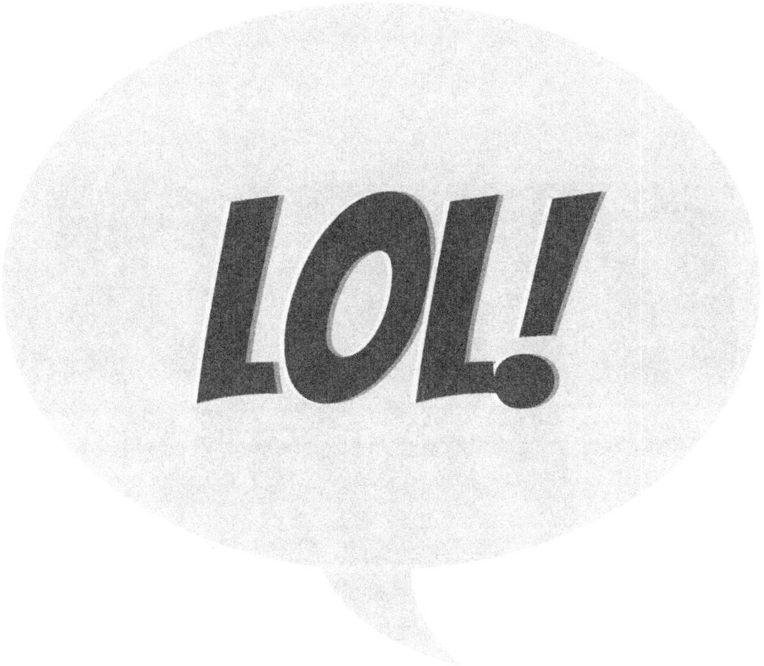
LOL!

LITTLE OLD LADY

LAUGHING MY DENTURES OUT

DRIVING WHILE INCONTINENT

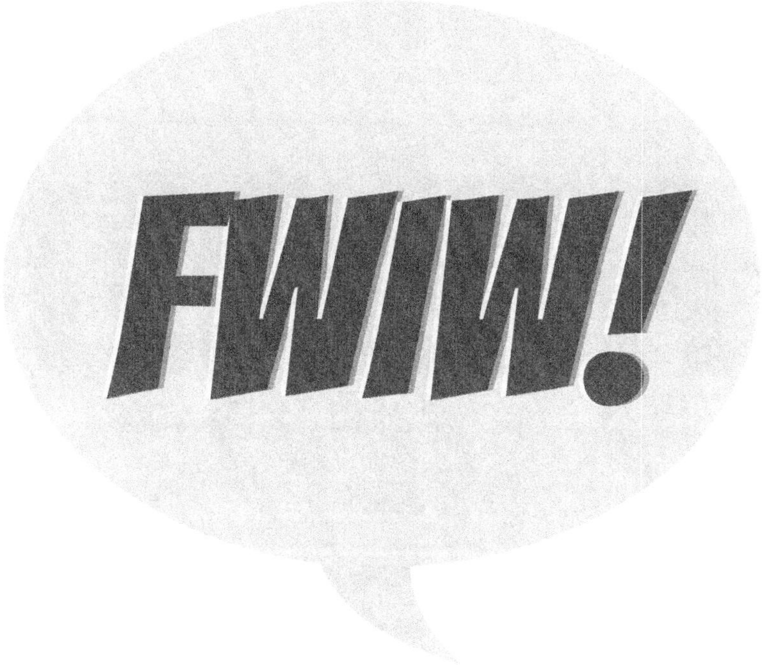
FWIW!

FORGOT WHERE I WAS

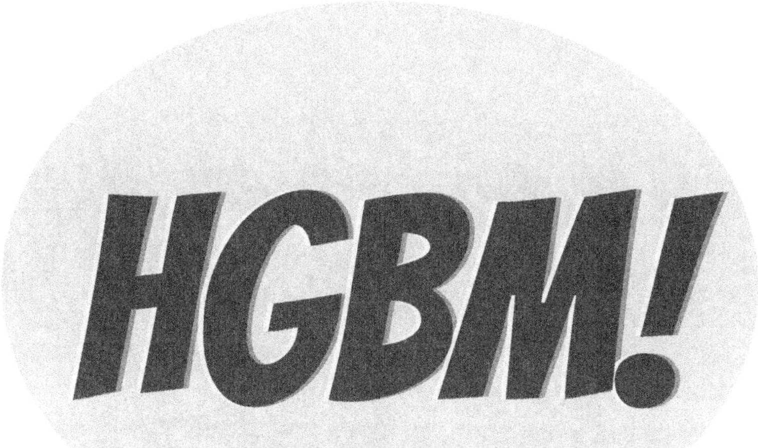
HGBM!

HAD GOOD BOWEL MOVEMENT

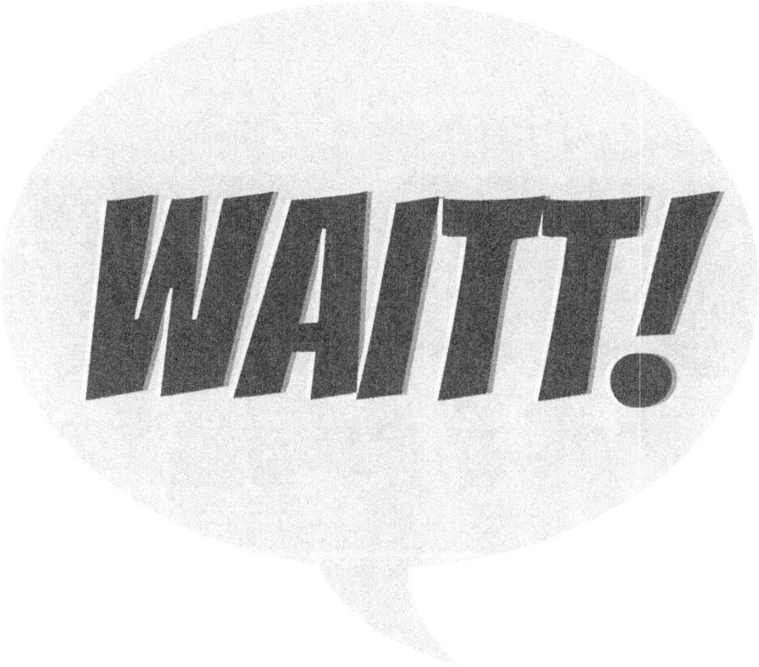
WAITT!

WHO AM I TALKING TO?

BEST FRIEND'S FUNERAL

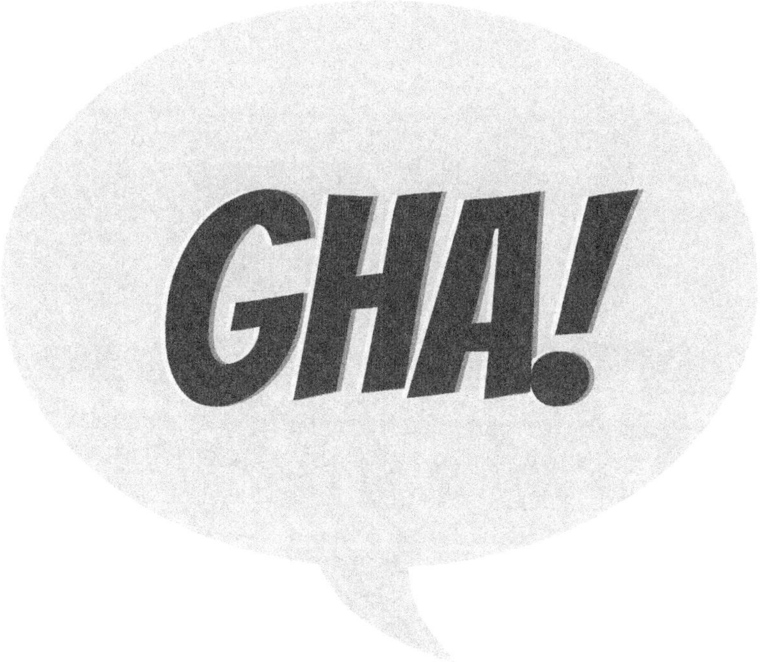
GHA!

GOT HEARTBURN AGAIN

IS MY HEARING-AID ON?

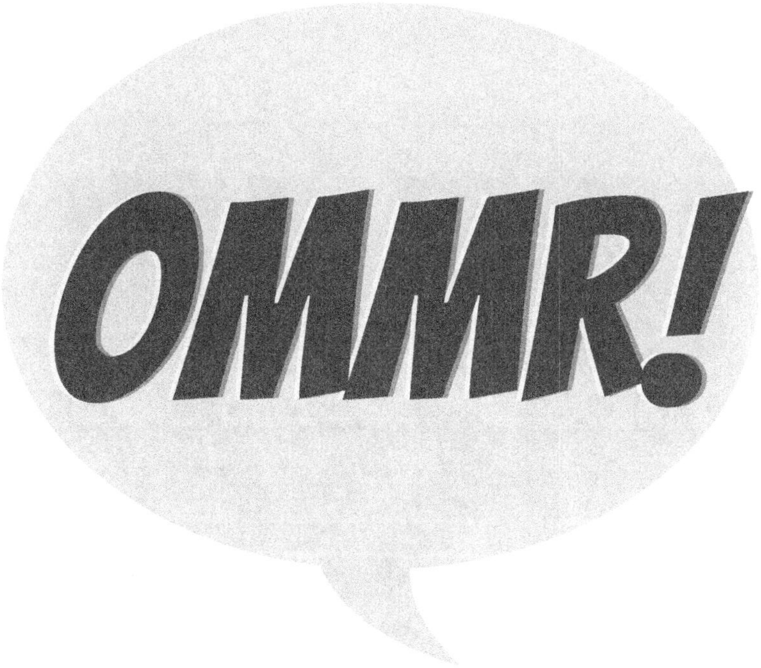
OMMR!

ON MY MASSAGE RECLINER

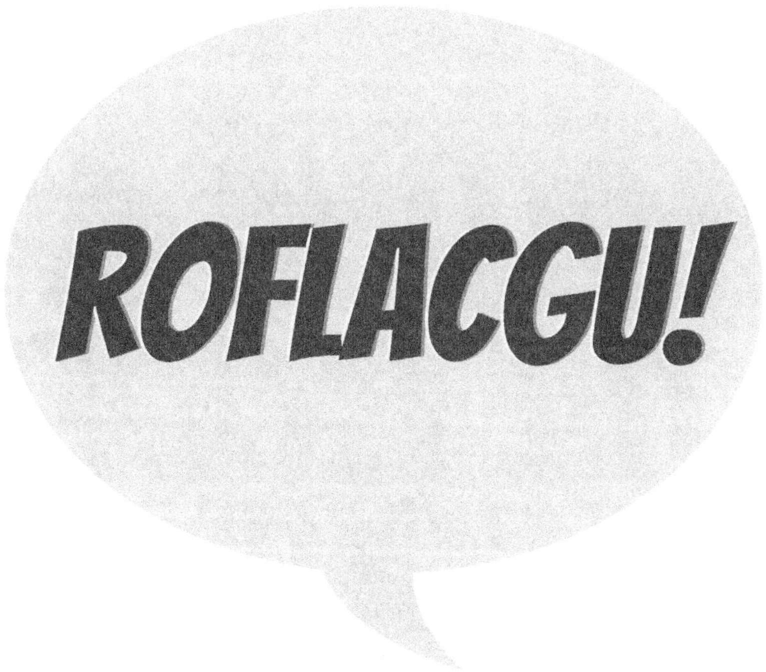
ROFLACGU!

ROLLING ON THE FLOOR LAUGHING, CAN'T GET UP

TTML!

TALK TO ME LOUDER

BRING THE WHEELCHAIR

AT THE DOCTORS

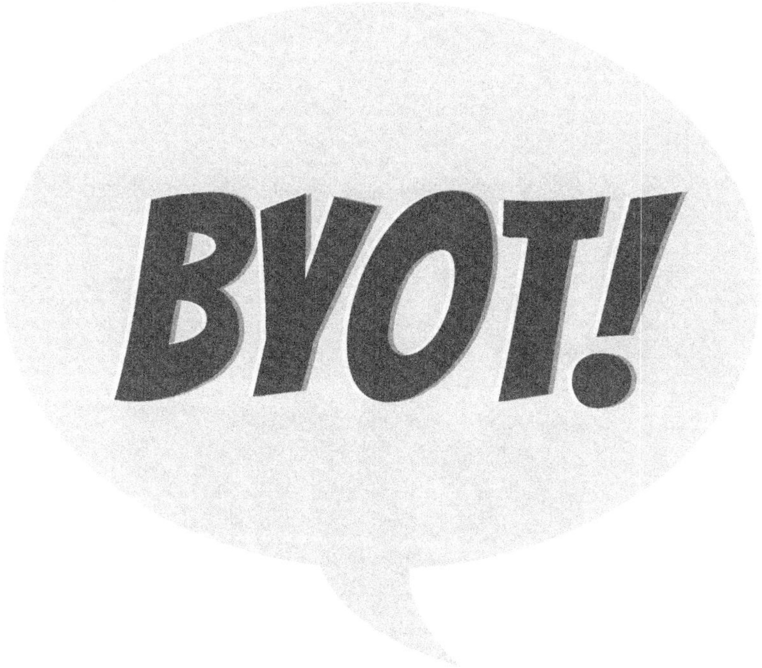
BYOT!

BRING YOUR OWN TEETH

WET THE FURNITURE AGAIN

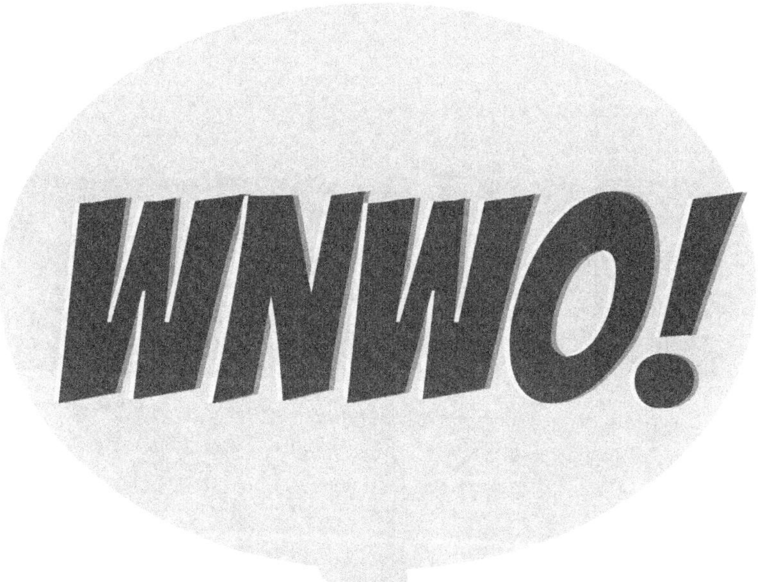
WNWO!

WALKER NEEDS WHEEL OIL

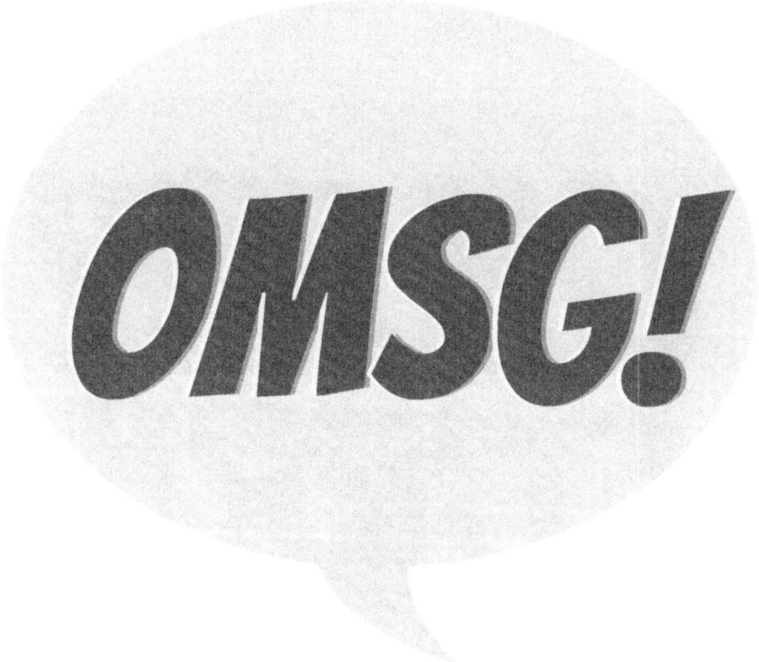
OMSG!

OH MY! SORRY, GAS

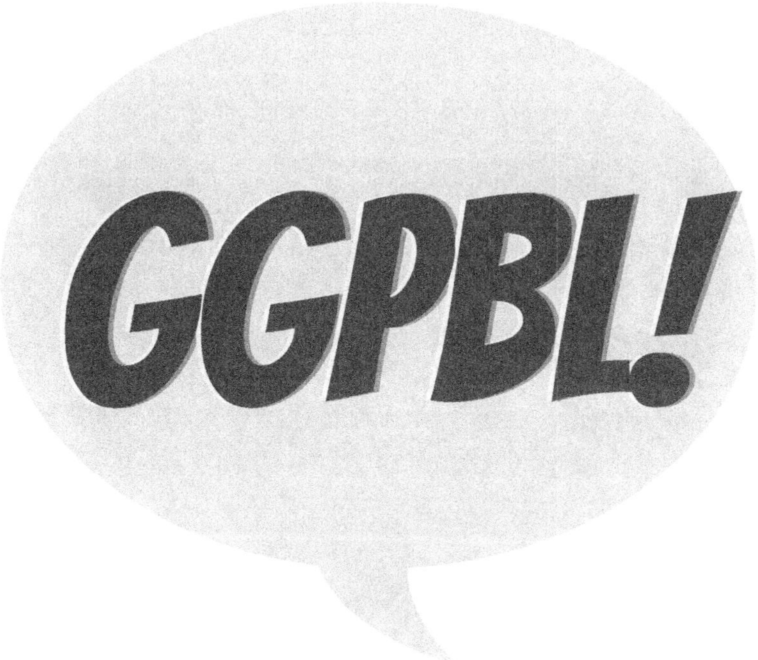
GGPBL!

GOTTA GO, PACEMAKER BATTERY LOW

FOUND MY INSULIN

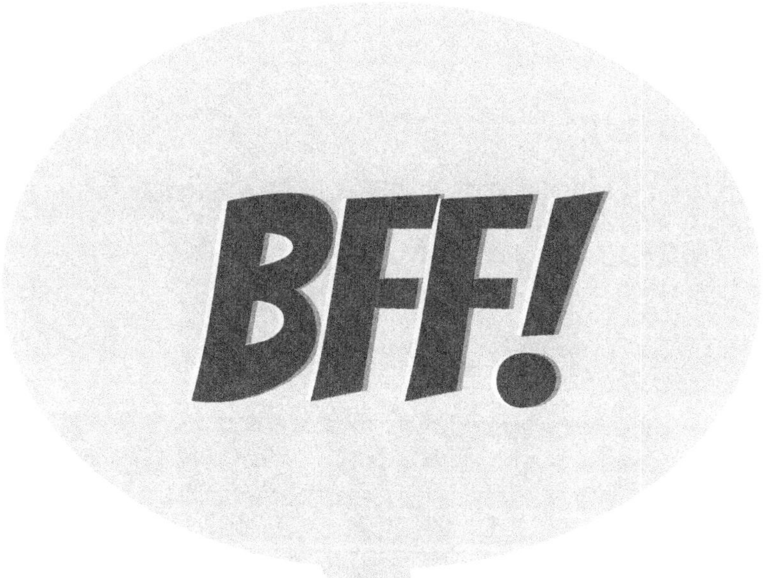
BFF!

BEST FRIEND FELL

ANY OTHER SENIOR'S TEXTING CODES?

ANY OTHER SENIOR'S TEXTING CODES?